A HUNDRED YEARS
AT WADDESDON

MARK GIROUARD

Frontispiece

The rooms at Waddesdon Manor reflect the eclectic taste
of Baron Ferdinand. He combined works of art of different types,
periods and sources to perfection in his arrangements of
historic furniture, paintings, textiles, porcelain and bronzes,
all of the highest quality.

Published 1998 by Rothschild Waddesdon Ltd.

ISBN 0 952 7809 25

Text by Mark Girouard
Edited by Ulrich Leben and Robert Selbie
© 1998 Designed and produced by Editions Quatre Fleuves,
75017 Paris
Typesetting by Ça ira ! Paris
Colour reproduction by PPC, Paris
Printed and bound by Proost, Belgium

CONTENTS

Chapter 1
The Rothschilds and their Houses   5

Chapter 2
Baron Ferdinand de Rothschild   13

Chapter 3
The Building of Waddesdon   19

Chapter 4
Life at Waddesdon   37

Chapter 5
Miss Alice   49

Chapter 6
James and Dorothy de Rothschild   57

Chapter 7
Lord Rothschild and
the Centenary Restoration   63

Bibliography and notes   80

Lord Rothschild commissioned the painter Jean Marc Winckler to paint a family tree showing the Rothschilds as builders. Forty two of the houses built by them throughout Europe during the nineteenth and early twentieth centuries are shown in the picture.

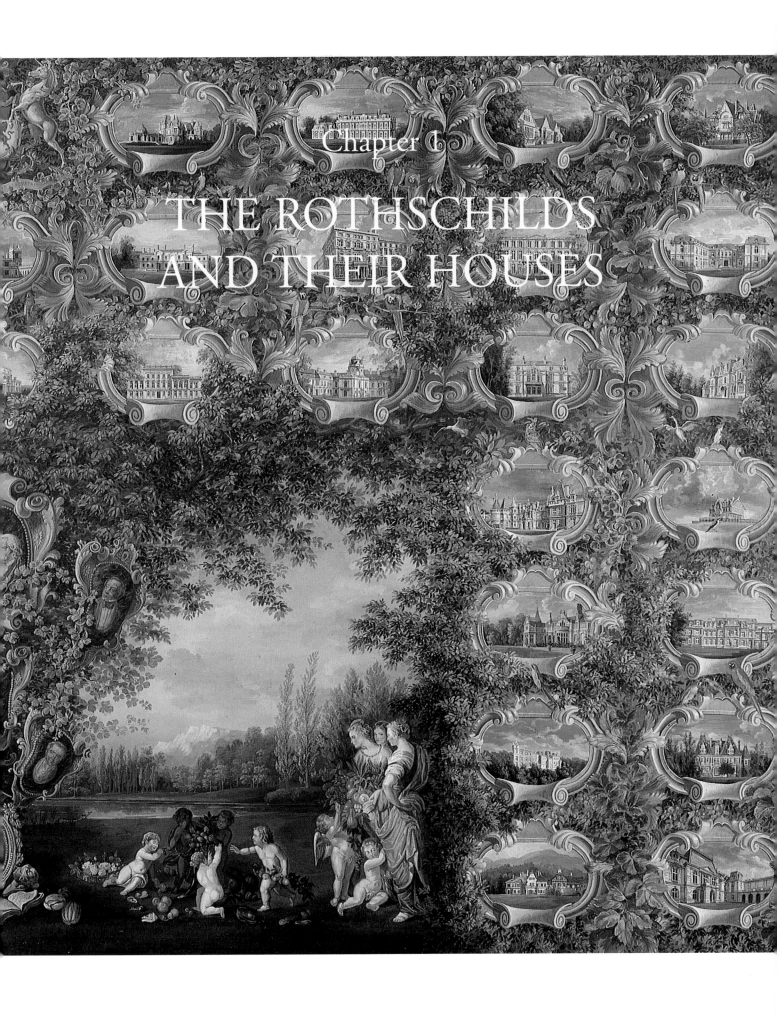

Chapter 1

THE ROTHSCHILDS
AND THEIR HOUSES

Right: The North Front of the house photographed around 1910.

Below: Waddesdon is one of the last remaining Rothschild houses open to the public with its contents intact and constantly being added to.

The foundation stone of Baron Ferdinand de Rothschild's enormous mansion at Waddesdon was laid on 9th August 1877. One hundred years earlier his great-grand father Mayer Amschel Rothschild occupied a narrow four-storey house in the Judengasse in Frankfurt. His ancestors had lived since at least the sixteenth century in this long canyon of timber and tile-hung houses, to which all Jews in Frankfurt were confined by law. He himself earned a modest income buying and selling coins, cloth, tobacco, wine and anything else out of which he could make a profit.

The Five Arrows

The seed of the family's international flowering was sown in 1769, when Mayer Amschel was appointed Crown Agent to Prince William of Hesse-Cassel, part of whose principality adjoined Frankfurt and whose family had grown rich out of supplying mercenaries to the rest of Europe. The appointment was relatively unimportant to begin with, but it led to the Rothschilds gradually taking over the management of the Prince's finances. The access to capital which this provided, the opportunities of the French wars, when governments needed loans and

Left: The South Front of the house around 1910.

Below: A modern view of the house photographed from the south.

armies pay on an unprecedented scale, the outstanding ability of Mayer Amschel and his five sons and their good judgement in backing the winning side, combined to make them rich, powerful, and famous. The device of five linked arrows, which they adopted as their crest in 1822, stood for the five brothers, sent from Frankfurt to establish banking houses all over Europe. Nathan Mayer moved to Manchester in 1798 and London in 1805, James to Paris in 1811, Carl to Naples and Salomon to Vienna in 1821. Amschel, the eldest, ran the parent bank in Frankfurt.

The five brothers worked closely together, built up an unequalled intelligence network, combined when appropriate to arrange loans or conduct deals, and became invaluable to governments all over Europe. All five brothers were created barons by the Emperor of Austria in 1822, by which time they were probably the richest family not of noble blood in Europe - and richer than many royal dynasties.

Houses and Collections
In the mid-century the Rothschilds continued to make money, and began to enjoy spending it. All but James, the youngest of the

five brothers, were dead by 1855; James lived on until 1868 and joined with the third generation to establish a new family pattern. Rothschilds now built houses in preference to buying them. They became collectors on an increasing scale, to fill and furnish their houses. They bought vineyards and kept racehorses. Some continued to work in their banks, but others lived lavishly on their unearned income and moved freely from country to country and from capital to capital. Rothschilds constantly met, corresponded, stayed with and above all married other Rothschilds. Of the eighteen Rothschild members of the third generation who reached maturity fourteen married Rothschilds, as did thirteen of the thirty-six equivalent Rothschilds of the fourth generation. The complications of the resulting inter-relationships defy analysis.

Left: Mentmore Towers, built by Joseph Paxton in 1850 for Mayer de Rothschild, is one of the earliest of a group of houses built for different members of the family in Buckinghamshire during the second half of the nineteenth century.

Above: James de Rothschild, of the French branch of the family, commissioned Joseph Paxton to design Ferrières, 1855 to 1863. He was instructed to build '... a Mentmore, only grander'.

A view of Miss Alice's drawing room on the first floor, in a coloured diascope photograph dating from 1910, showing an arrangement in 'Rothschild taste'.

The first major house to be built by the family was Mentmore in Buckinghamshire, designed by Joseph Paxton and his future son-in-law G.H. Stokes in 1850 for Baron Nathan Mayer de Rothschild, of the English branch. By the end of the century over sixty houses had been built throughout Europe by different members of the family in different countries and capitals, many on a palatial scale.

Stylistically, the houses showed considerable diversity, especially on the exterior. Mentmore was closely modelled on the Elizabethan Wollaton Hall in Nottinghamshire; Ferrières, which Paxton and Stokes built for James de Rothschild in 1854-59, was similar in character, but rather more French and Italian than Elizabethan, and even larger. The two huge palaces which Ferdinand de Rothschild's brothers built in Vienna in the 1870s were designed by the French architects Jean Girette and Gabriel-Hippolyte Destailleur in a style closely modelled on French seventeenth and eighteenth century prototypes; but the Schloss Waidhofen, in Lower Austria, was Gothic by Friedrich von Schmidt, 1885-7 and so was De Haar, the enormous castle built in Holland in 1892 by the Dutch architect Petrus Hubertus Cuypers for Baron van Zuylen and paid for by his Rothschild wife. Ascott in Buckinghamshire, built by Leopold de Rothschild to the designs of George Devey in the 1870s, was a half-timbered so-called 'cottage' on a more than generous scale; and the London mansion built by Lionel de Rothschild in Piccadilly, next to Apsley House, in the 1860s was designed by Charles Innes and Thomas Marsh Nelson in the Renaissance palazzo style.

A characteristic aspect of the arrangement of the Collection at Waddesdon. In front of the eighteenth century panelling is a French commode by Charles Cressent, on its marble top stands a statue of Mercury by the French sculptor J.B. Pigalle.

'Rothschild taste'

There was great diversity inside the houses as well, but they had enough in common to give birth to the phrase 'le goût Rothschild'. Opulence was the key-note of this, an opulence of marble, bronze, gilt, and crystal chandeliers, but above all one made up of old rather than contemporary contents and fittings: most notably, although by no means exclusively, of eighteenth-century French furniture, porcelain and bronzes of superb quality combined, at least from the 1850s, with French boiseries and chimneypieces.

The first great Rothschild collector was Baron Nathan Mayer. He started buying in the 1840s and not only filled Mentmore with his purchases but combined its neo-Elizabethan façades with a series of rooms which were, as the periodical 'The Builder' put it in 1857, *...elaborately finished and decorated according to the styles which prevailed in France during the reigns of Kings François I and Louis XIV, Louis XV, and Louis XVI... .*

When Ferdinand de Rothschild visited Alnwick Castle in 1864, shortly after it had been remodelled and redecorated by the 4th Duke of Northumberland, he wrote to his uncle: ... *I cannot say that I found the decoration of the rooms very tasteful, though they are extremely gorgeous and must have cost hundreds of thousands ... everything is modern, including the furniture, and I think that you will agree with me in not much admiring entire new sets of boulle and marquetry cabinets. My cicerone informed me that there were some old pictures and furniture, but that they were stored away... .(1)*

Alnwick represented what was still the prevailing tradition: a rich man building a new house or remodelling an old one would buy new furniture, new porcelain, new carpets, new fittings, and very often new pictures and sculpture with which to furnish it. That was not the Rothschilds' way; they played almost no part as patrons of contemporary art and design. In collecting objects from former times they were by no means pioneers, however. The tradition of collecting non-contemporary pictures and sculpture went back to the sixteenth century; in the late eighteenth and early nineteenth centuries antiquaries had inaugurated a fashion for collecting old furniture, woodwork and panelling. Patrons and collectors like the Prince Regent, William Beckford and the Marquis of Hertford became avid buyers of earlier French furniture, encouraged by the amount that was coming onto the market as the result of the French

The Starhemberg service in its cases - custom made for every piece of the dinner service - shows the particular care which all members of the Rothschild family took of their collections.

Right: A bronze clock, from about 1770, called *pendule à la Geoffrin,* after the famous Parisian hostess who was one of the early commissioners of the model. Ferdinand's clock is reputed to have come from the collection of Horace Walpole at Strawberry Hill .

Below: The panelling of the Green Boudoir came from the town house of the banker Pierre Dodin in the rue Richelieu in Paris. The work in this house was carried out under the supervision of the architect Jean-Baptiste Bullet de Chamblin between 1725 and 1727.

Revolution and subsequent European upheavals. In the 1820s this interest stimulated a revival of opulent interior decoration in the French style - sometimes, as at Windsor and Belvoir Castles, incorporating French eighteenth century wall panelling.

'Curiosities'

The Rothschilds moved into the market for what were known at the time as 'curiosities' rather than 'antiques' in the 1840s. In the 1870s they came to dominate that market in Europe through their number and their enthusiasm, their increasing knowledge, their apparently limitless resources. They became compulsive collectors, who could not only afford to buy the best but to buy it by the dozen and the hundred; as Ferdinand put it in 1874, writing about his Parisian cousin Alphonse: *...I never saw a prettier table*

than Alphonse's - it actually groaned under the weight of green Sèvres... .

The three brothers, Barons Alphonse, Gustave and Edmond, were first cousins of Ferdinand, and all partners in the Paris bank. Gustave and Edmond were creating splendid houses in Paris at much the same time as their cousin at Waddesdon, and were buying indefatigably to furnish them. Other Rothschilds, including Baron Charles from Frankfurt and Baron Ferdinand's brothers, Nathaniel and Albert, from Vienna were often to be found *'curiosity hunting'* in Paris. As in their business deals, the cousinhood sometimes joined together for a big purchase; in 1874 Alphonse shared with Ferdinand a collection of Sèvres bought from Madame Oger, and the super Van Loon collection of Dutch paintings was bought jointly in 1877 by five Rothschilds,

Left: View of Baron Ferdinand's private sitting room showing the harmonious late nineteenth century arrangement of historic furniture and *objets d'art.*

Below: The marble group *Allegory of Architecture and Geometry* by Jean-Jacques Caffieri in the East Gallery. It belonged originally to the Abbé Terray in the sale of whose effects in 1779 the group is first documented.

including Ferdinand. But on the whole they operated individually and, as in all closely-knit families, an enjoyable amount of gossip and rivalry was generated as they bought and built. The flavour of their activities comes across strongly in Ferdinand's letters. A Sèvres table *...had been purchased at Biarritz for £2000 by some dealers...,* of which Edmond is now the *...happy possessor ...but at what price I don't know... .* Gustave is seriously contemplating the purchase of some *...well-known boiseries...* Alphonse *...has taken a French curiosity dealer with him to Vienna to ferret out things for him there... .* He supposes that Gustave and Edmond *...want to astonish us when their houses are finished...,* but Gustave's *...will be a good place for draughts...,* and about Edmond's new house *...there is not that echo of admiration on the part of Alphonse which you would expect to come from a brother's heart...* In general *...my dearly beloved relatives continue purchasing artistic wonders. Oddly enough, they never admire each other's purchases....* Adolphe *...says that all Charles' marvels are more or less objects which the Paris Gentleman and himself would not purchase... .* Alphonse has bought an unique reliquary: *...I should think it would make both Baron Charles and Adolphe rather green and yellow... .* In Paris *...I saw a very pretty Louis XVI mantelpiece for which I offered five thousand francs, and which Gustave bought five minutes afterwards, for twelve... .* Although competition from non-Rothschild buyers was growing, and *...everyone is running about like wild for things... it is wonderful how much there is still left, and there is no fear that for many years to come the Rothschilds will be prevented from increasing their collections... .*(2)

BARON FERDINAND
DE ROTHSCHILD

Previous page: Baron Ferdinand with his favourite French poodle Poupon.

Left: Baron Ferdinand as a Member of Parliament. The watercolour, signed Hay, was published as a lithograph in 1889 in *Vanity Fair.*

He was always comfortably off, and the death of his father in 1874 made him extremely rich. As a young man he worked competently in the Viennese bank, but after his marriage and inheritance he was able to devote his time to travelling, building, collecting and political activities.

The collector

He was fluent in three languages and as much at home in Paris as in London. Inspired by his father, he was already a collector in his early twenties; his first purchase was made when he was 21, a turquoise Sèvres 'boat shaped' potpourri vase which he bought by instalments and which is still at Waddesdon. He developed a passion for collecting outstanding even among Rothschilds, so that family letters are full of references to his *...curiosity-hunting...* all over Europe. It was inevitable that he would build a house in the end, and Waddesdon was typical of Rothschild houses in its eclecticism and the nature of its contents, even if it outdid them all in quality and splendour.

His first cousin Constance Flower (later Lady Battersea) visited it in August 1880 when it was in course of being built; she could not fail to be impressed, but commented in her diary: *...think the scheme a mad one...* . She had in mind, perhaps, the contrast between the gigantic building and the slight and rather lonely figure of the

Ferdinand de Rothschild epitomised the expanding life style of the fourth generation. He was born in Paris in 1839, the son of a Viennese and an English Rothschild, Anselm Salomon and Charlotte. He moved to England in 1860, married his English Rothschild cousin Evelina in 1865, and continued to live there after she and her baby died in childbirth in 1866. In her memory he founded the Evelina Hospital for Children in Southwark, and the Evelina Rothschild Ward in the Royal Bucks Hospital, Aylesbury.

Above: Historic view of the Manor. The North Front with a marquee for tea on the lawn.

Below: The turquoise blue porcelain ship by the Sèvres factory dates from the mid-eighteenth century and was one of Baron Ferdinand's first acquisitions, in 1861. He was particularly fond of this piece.

childless widower, for and by whom it was being built.

A frugal and reserved gentleman

There was nothing flamboyant, exhibitionist or ebullient about Baron Ferdinand. He was a shy and reserved man, who suffered from wretched health and a melancholy which was accentuated by the death of his wife and child. The Irish M.P. T.P. O'Connor saw in him *...a good deal of that joylessness which is so often the sad heritage of a long line of wealthy ancestors...*, and his friend Sir Edward Hamilton thought that *...though he had everything that wealth could give him, yet owing to his weak-*

ly health and the solitude in which he lived in his splendid home, I doubt if he was ever a really happy man... .

He lived on his nerves. He was impatient and easily bored. As Edward Hamilton put it: *...he was always in a hurry. He did not eat, but devoured. He did not walk but ran through galleries and places to be seen. He could not wait for anybody or anything. He played three games of patience when most people would be playing one... .*

His tastes were frugal. O'Connor thought him *...as much an ascetic as if he were bound by vows. An occasional cigarette was his one strong*

A photograph in the Red Book showing Baron Ferdinand in his private sitting room with his poodle, Poupon. Remarkably little has changed since this picture was taken more than a hundred years ago.

indulgence... . He sat in the middle of his huge house-party dinners at Waddesdon drinking water and eating toast. He was a teetotaller and a supporter of the Temperance Movement but neither in this nor in any other respect did he attempt to force his views on other people. He lectured on Temperance and supported a Temperance Silver Band in the village but, unlike many teetotal landlords, he supplied it with a superb new public house, suitably named 'The Five Arrows'.

He also lectured, in the village and in Aylesbury, on eighteenth-century subjects such as the French Revolution, George III and John Wilkes. He was widely read, especially in eighteenth century French and English memoirs. His lectures were privately prin-

In 1898 Baron Ferdinand gave his collection of European *Kunstkammer* objects to the British Museum in London where it is now shown as the Waddesdon Bequest.

The Five Arrows Hotel was built in 1887 for Baron Ferdinand by the Bierton architects W.Taylor and Son, using local stone and brick with Monk's Park stone dressing.

ted, along with a book of essays, a lively account of a visit to South Africa, and a short (and not very good) Eastern tale, published anonymously.

He was M.P. for Aylesbury from 1885 until his death, and a Trustee of the British Museum for the last two years of his life. According to contemporary commentaries Baron Ferdinand ...*was an extremely popular man*... however he never lived in any sense as a public figure. Although his literary work is by no means despicable, his letters - a little formal but never pompous, full of gossip and seasoned by an agreeably astringent sense of humour - give a better idea of his personality.

As a young man he was an enthusiastic fox-hunter, but his health made him give up hunting shortly after he moved into Waddesdon. His other main interests were his collections, his friends, his animals, and the creation and running of Waddesdon. Its contents, and the Waddesdon Bequest in the British Museum, are the memorial to his genius as a collector. As a friend, although by nature touchy and quick to take offence, he gave and inspired great affection. In 1878 he wrote to his cousin and one of his closest friends, Lord Rosebery: ...*I am a lonely, suffering and occasionally a very miserable individual, despite the gilded and marbled rooms in which I live - there is but one thing in the world that I care for, and that is the sympathy and the confi-*

Apart from dogs and birds Baron Ferdinand kept many other animals on the Estate, such as llamas and deer. They all knew him and were not afraid of him.

dence of the few persons whom I love... .(3)
He adored his animals. *...Every day at Waddesdon...*, according to an obituary, *...despite wind and weather, he went round and fed with his own hand the deer, the llamas, the wild sheep, and the gaily plumaged birds. They all knew him, and great was the commotion when his spare, delicate figure was seen approaching, accompanied by his burly bailiff, and preceded by his French poodle 'Poupon'. This clever dog was his one constant companion for the past eight years... .(4)*

He had a gift for large-scale and complex organisation which might have made him a

fortune had he needed to make one. As it was, it was deployed on the building and running of Waddesdon and on entertaining on the grand scale there, in his house in London and, in the last years of his life, on his fine steam yacht the Rona. Superb organisation was combined with a sense of style and quality. Everything was of the best: materials, furniture, porcelain, food and flowers, brought together with apparently effortless efficiency by the best servants, for the enjoyment of the best people.

Opposite: The inspiration from the château of Blois is easily recognised in this drawing by the architect Destailleur for the staircase at Waddesdon.

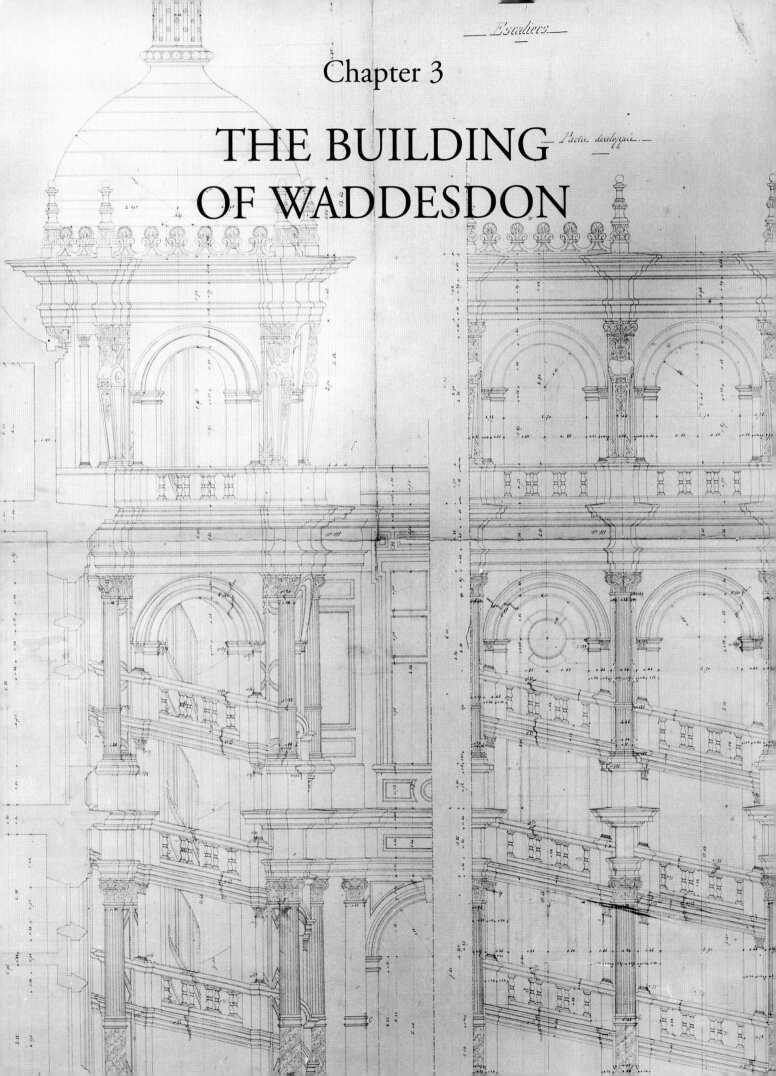

Chapter 3

THE BUILDING OF WADDESDON

In London the Rothschilds lived close to each other in and around Piccadilly; in the country they colonised the Vale of Aylesbury. The move to Buckinghamshire was started when Mayer and his brother bought the Mentmore and Aston Clinton estates in 1848 and 1853. A second wave of settlement came in the 1870s. Ferdinand's father-in-law, Lionel, bought the Tring estate in 1872 and the Halton estate (where his son was to build a great house in the 1880s) in 1853. Leopold's house at Ascott was built on property bought by Mayer in 1874. Ferdinand began by renting houses for the hunting, first one at Wing and then Leighton House, on the main street of Leighton Buzzard, in 1874 or a little earlier. In the same year he bought the Waddesdon estate, and his sister Alice bought the adjacent Eythrope estate in 1875. These estate purchases were not inexpensive despite the agricultural depression which only affected prices at the very end of the decade. In fact they were purchased at, or near, the top of the market.

The site of Waddesdon

Baron Ferdinand bought Waddesdon without seeing it, at least with a view to purchase; he had hunted around and perhaps over the estate, and noticed the treeless eminence known as Lodge Hill which was its most prominent feature, before its owner, the 7th Duke of Marlborough, put the property on the market. It was auctioned on 7th July 1874, but failed to reach its reserve. Baron Ferdinand's father, Anselm, died in Frankfurt on 27th July. Ferdinand had gone out to him a few days before his death. The Aylesbury solicitor James James, who was the agent and confidential advisor to all the Rothschilds over Buckinghamshire matters, went out to Frankfurt to consult him, and returned to buy Waddesdon by private treaty in his absence, some time in the first half of August. Baron Ferdinand looked at his new property for the first time on 1st September, and wrote to his father-in-law: ...*I hasten to tell you that I am very much pleased with it - I think it a lovely tract of land, beautiful soil, a few capital covers and very pretty sce-*

BUCKS.

Particulars and Conditions of Sale

OF A VERY IMPORTANT

FREEHOLD

MANORIAL ESTATE,

PRINCIPALLY TITHE FREE AND LAND TAX REDEEMED,

Situate about Five Miles and a Half from Aylesbury, only One Mile from the Quainton Station of the Aylesbury and Buckingham Railway, and Twelve from Buckingham;

COMPRISING THE

MANOR OF OVER WINCHENDON, the MANOR OR LORDSHIP OF WADDESDON and also the MANOR OF WESTCOTT,

WITH THEIR RIGHTS, MEMBERS, AND APPURTENANCES THERETO BELONGING;

SEVERAL FARMS,

KNOWN AS

MAINS HILL, LINCE, UPPER WINCHENDON, DECOY, WINDMILL HILL, COM Leys, Westcott Field, Lodge Hill, and Westcott;

WITH

SUPERIOR FARM RESIDENCES,

AND VERY

EXTENSIVE AND APPROPRIATE FARM BUILDINGS,

The "CROOKED BILLET" Public House, situate at Ham Green; and the "MARLBOROUGH ARMS," in the Village of Waddesdon; about

FIFTY COTTAGES,

AND

SUNDRY ENCLOSURES OF ACCOMMODATION LAND,

THE WHOLE WITHIN A RING FENCE.

Except as to a small part, in and near the Villages of Waddesdon and Westcott, in one of the finest Dairy Districts in the County.

THE WHOLE EMBRACES AN AREA OF ABOUT

TWO THOUSAND SEVEN HUNDRED & SIXTY-TWO ACRES

And producing, independent of the Valuable Woods in hand, a present inadequate Rental of nearly

£5800. PER ANNUM.

Which will be Sold by Auction,

BY MESSRS.

FAREBROTHER, CLARK & CO.

At the Auction Mart, Tokenhouse Yard, Lothbury, E.C.

On TUESDAY, the 7th day of JULY, 1874,

AT ONE FOR TWO O'CLOCK.

The Waddesdon Estate was put up for sale by the Duke of Marlborough in 1874. The Estate consisted not only of Lodge Hill on which the Manor was later built but also a number of farms, cottages and village houses.

Waddesdon Manor seen from Upper Winchendon looks like a vision of a romantic castle. Before the Manor was built, the hill was almost bare of trees, as can still be seen today in the neighbouring hills of Quainton, Ashendon or Brill. Baron Ferdinand planted fully grown trees in order to create an appropriate setting for the dramatic architecture of his French château in Buckinghamshire.

nery - the only thing it seems to be deficient in is timber... . The deficiency was soon, and dramatically, to be remedied. (5)

The estate consisted of 2,762 acres, to which the Baron added about 500 over the years. It included the villages of Winchendon and Waddesdon, but there was no big house on it. Although the Baron decided from the beginning that the top of Lodge Hill was the site on which to build one, it was to be nearly three years before the foundation stone was laid. The interval was spent commissio-

ning designs, arranging for a water supply, and preparing the ground. Water was brought sixteen miles, at the Baron's expense, from the Chiltern Hill Water Company Works, the nearest point high enough to provide the pressure necessary to work fountains at Waddesdon.

A French Renaissance château in Buckinghamshire

Baron Ferdinand wrote his own account of the creation of Waddesdon in the volume of photographs and accompanying text known

Left: Baron Ferdinand asked the architect Destailleur to take his inspiration for Waddesdon from the castles of the Loire in France. The famous staircase of Blois, dated 1515-1524, served as an example for the design of the stairway towers at Waddesdon Manor.

Centre: Destailleur was inspired by Chambord to build the beautifully carved chimneys and roof ornaments at Waddesdon.

Below: The château of Mouchy which was rebuilt on medieval foundations by Destailleur for the Mouchy family.

as the 'Red Book', which he had printed for private circulation in 1897: *...As soon as the contract was signed, I set out for Paris in quest of an architect... having been greatly impressed by the ancient châteaux of the Valois during a tour I once made in Touraine, I determined to build my house in the same style, and considered it safer to get the designs made by a French architect who was familiar with the work ... The French six-teenth-century style, on which I had long set my heart, was particularly suitable to the sur-roundings of the site I had selected, and more uncommon than the Tudor, Jacobean or Adam, of which the country affords so many and such unique specimens... .* (6)
Perhaps 'more uncommon' rather than 'parti-

cularly suitable' is the important phrase. It is hard to see why the Baron thought a French Renaissance château was suitable for a Buckinghamshire hilltop, but it was certainly uncommon and moreover had not been tried by other Rothschilds. A French architect was called for, but not one who designed in the lush contemporary classicism of the Second Empire; the Baron disapproved of this, and considered the Paris Opera House, the style's most famous example, *...frightfully overdo-ne... .* The Rothschilds had worked against Napoleon I, had never been easy with Napoleon III, and had been bitter rivals of Emile Pereire, the financier behind Second Empire improvements in Paris. They had established a close relationship with the last

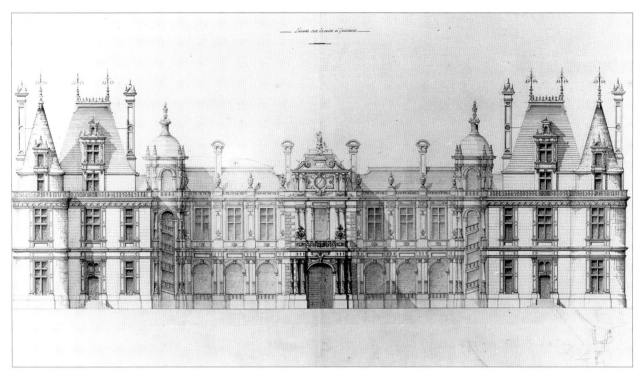

A drawing showing the North Front with the main entrance to the house. The preparatory drawings for Waddesdon Manor have survived at the Academie d'Architecture in Paris and at the Kunstbibliothek in Berlin.

Bourbons, as they had with others of the traditional royal houses in Europe. Waddesdon can be seen as a deliberate reaction against Napoleonic modernism, using elements from royal châteaux of past centuries to set off contents also of past centuries, and often also of royal origin.

A French architect: Gabriel-Hippolyte-Alexandre Destailleur

With these requirements, the choice of architect almost inevitably fell on Gabriel-Hippolyte-Alexandre Destailleur. The architect's father and grandfather had been architects to the Dukes of Orleans. He was recognised as France's leading consultant for the restoration or extension of historic châteaux, or the building of new houses closely based

on historic styles. His knowledge was grounded on what was probably the largest collection of French architectural books and engravings assembled by a private individual in the nineteenth century. His best known restoration was that of the château de Mouchy near Beauvais (1858-68). His new buildings, prior to Waddesdon, included the hôtel de Behague in Paris (1872) and the palais Pless in Berlin (1872-75), in both of which he reused eighteenth-century fittings. His work at Waddesdon led to a commission to design a great house on the Prinz-Eugen-Strasse, Vienna. This was built for Ferdinand's brother Albert around a reconstruction of the Escalier des Ambassadeurs at the château at Versailles.

Built between 1874-84 it was damaged in the

Above: The staircase tower as it was built is reminiscent of the château of Blois.

Right: Destailleur's preparatory drawing for the staircase tower.

World War II, and was subsequently demolished. In 1880 he also designed a town house in London for Ferdinand's cousin Lord Rose-bery, which was never built. Between 1882 and 1887 he built the great French Gothic revival mausoleum at Farnborough, a commission by the former Empress Eugenie who after 1871 had emigrated from France.

Destailleur made a series of designs for Waddesdon at the end of 1874 and early 1875. They were closely related to the house that was finally built, but had much larger wings, advancing to either side of the staircase towers to enclose a forecourt. Baron Ferdinand described the result as *...on a scale of such grandeur that I begged him to reduce it...* . The architect acted accordingly to Ferdinand's wish, remarking *...you will regret your decision ... one always builds too small...* . And indeed the house was substantially enlarged in 1888-91 by the addition of the Morning Room Wing to the west and the enlargement of the East Wing to contain a Smoking Room and extra bedrooms. Destailleur retired in about 1890, and the practice was taken over by his son Walter-André. (7)

Exterior Style

Destailleur gave the Baron exactly what he wanted: an anthology of quotations from a wide variety of French châteaux, skilfully adapted and combined to make one overpowering whole. The high-roofed and machicolated wings that enclose and frame the lower and more richly decorated centre derive from early sixteenth century châteaux, especially Maintenon and Chaumont. The central range draws on later sixteenth and early seventeenth-century sources; its richness and symmetry give a foretaste of the splendour and formal planning of the great reception rooms inside it. The staircases which feature so distinctively on the entrance front are reminiscent (as Baron Ferdinand states) of the famous open staircase at Blois, but in fact are much closer to similar but slightly later

The East Staircase as it is today with its original red carpet.

staircases at Chambord, which are glazed like those at Waddesdon. The chimneystacks derive from those originally on the Lescot wing of the Louvre, the lead dome of the central roof from the early seventeenth century Pavillon de l'Horloge at the Louvre, the dormer windows from Chenonceaux and Azay-le-Rideau. The central feature on the entrance front, with its circular window and split pediment and the Corinthian columns, with their partially carved drums, are based on Anet. These columns are regularly repeated along the central block on both floors and both sides as a unifying feature, and the whole building is united by continuous horizontal lines of entablature or machicolations running right the way round it. The later Morning Room Wing was originally designed as an elaborate confection of French Flamboyant Gothic; in the end the Gothic elements were much reduced, perhaps because it was felt that the variety of motifs was already sufficiently overpowering.

The first part of the house to be completed was the East or so-called Bachelors' Wing - rather confusingly named for, in addition to the Billiard Room and a run of bachelor

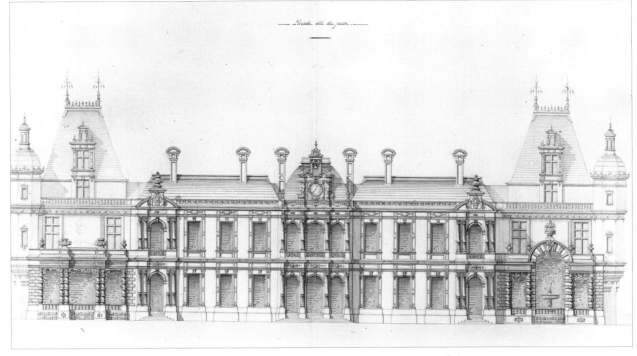

Above: An early design by Destailleur for the South Front or Garden Side of the Manor.

Below: A detail from a window in the roof showing the skilled carving by stone masons from the Paris workshop of Doumassy who had also worked for the Orleans family and at Mouchy.

bedrooms, it also contained the Kitchen, Servants' Hall, Still-Room, menservants' bedrooms and other service rooms. Baron Ferdinand entertained a small party of men-friends there in May 1880. The first house party in the main house took place in June 1883 and the official house warming, complete with a ball and a firework display, followed in July with the Prince of Wales among the guests.

The Baron probably always intended that the interiors of Waddesdon should be decorated in a number of different styles, after the manner of Mentmore. He may not have envisaged the predominance of eighteenth-century contents and panelling which the house finally acquired. But the full story is unlikely ever to be known because the building accounts, correspondence and drawings which must once have been there have all been lost or destroyed; and although a sizeable collection of Destailleur's

Left: The Smoking Room and its fireplace as finally built and shown here after the room was restored in 1997.

Right above: Drawing of an unrealised project for the Smoking Room.

Right: This drawing for a chimney shows the architect's skilful use of historical ornament, for which he was well known.

Waddesdon designs survives in the Archives Nationales in Paris and the Kunstbibliothek in Berlin, many of these are for projects or decoration which were never executed.

Internal decoration

According to the Baron's own account Destailleur *...took but a very small part...* in the internal decorations; panelling was purchased in Paris for several rooms *...to which it was adapted by various English and French decorators...*, who copied the ceilings in the houses from which the panelling came, or ceilings of similar date. (8) In fact Destailleur did more than the Baron suggested. He certainly designed the decorations of the Billiard Room, of the two staircases and of the Entrance Lobby and Vestibule. Billiard Room and staircases follow the French Renaissance style of the exterior of the house, but the Lobby and Vestibule are accomplished exercises based on mid-seventeenth-century French Classicism. The Dining Room is an equally accomplished and,

Above: House party given for the Prince of Wales, later Edward VII, in July 1894. From the time that the house was finished Baron Ferdinand brought his friends to Waddesdon for his famous house parties. The guest book, as well as a number of photographs taken on these occasions, give an impression of these events.

Left: The Red Drawing Room in an historic view from the Red Book. The large eighteenth century English portraits still occupy the same positions in which they were hung by Baron Ferdinand.

Above: The Grey Drawing Room. The collection of furniture and objects brought together by Baron Ferdinand and Miss Alice increased after 1934 when James de Rothschild inherited part of the collection of his father Baron Edmond.

Right: The Morning Room in a photograph from the Red Book. This room, built between 1888-1889, was intended as a meeting and writing room when Baron Ferdinand became a Member of Parliament.

because of its size and splendour, more spectacular amalgam of marble-lined rooms of the 1670s at Versailles, with rococo-revival plasterwork and French Rococo mirrors. The eclecticism and success of the design suggest Destailleur, but no drawings or identifiable payments have come to light.

Destailleur also provided a sizeable proportion of the period fittings: the sixteenth-century chimneypiece in the Billiard Room came through him, as did the eighteenth-century panelling in the Grey Drawing Room, the Breakfast Room, the Green Boudoir, and the East Gallery. The Destailleur archive includes a photograph of the chimneypiece, drawings for installing the Grey Drawing Room panelling (which came from a house in Paris belonging to the Order of the Sacré-Coeur, whose architect he was), and a floor plan of the house of the hôtel Dodun, the source of the panelling in the other three rooms. Destailleur had originally been planning to install panelling from Spain in the Red Drawing Room, but in 1881 decided against it, and wrote to Baron Ferdinand that *...panelling from Paris is in better taste... .(9)*

Surviving designs by Destailleur for the Red Drawing Room and Gallery do not correspond to what is there today; the former was to have been called the van Dyck Saloon, and was probably intended to centre round a full length copy of van Dyck's portrait of Prince Thomas of Savoy, which the Baron had bought in Genoa. Ultimately this was hung in an obscure position in the Bedroom Corridor - perhaps when it was discovered to be a copy.

The Stables on the North Drive down to the Dairy. The building was designed by Destailleur. The sculpture of a horse is by the Victorian sculptor Joseph Edgar Boehm and was cast in bronze by the London founders C.Broad and Son between 1888 and 1890.

The Glass Houses at Waddesdon Manor were famous as the largest privately owned glass houses in this country and provided fresh flowers and vegetables throughout the year.

At the end of his life Destailleur, in collaboration with his son, made designs for the Smoking Room, but these were much altered in execution by the Paris decorators Messieurs André, a firm which continued to be employed at Waddesdon for many years. *French decorators...*, according to the local paper, were responsible for a fire in the Morning Room Wing in 1891, which destroyed the Baron's best Gainsborough 'Sisters'. Payments in his account were made to the London decorators Charles Mellier and Co., of Margaret Street, and Thomas Kershaw, of Baker Street, but there is no evidence as to what these involved. (10)

The Stables were built in, or soon after, 1883 to Destailleur's designs for the external façades only. According to his grandson he had a hand in the enormous glasshouses, built by R. Halliday of Middleton, Yorkshire, which were one of the main features of Waddesdon, but which were demolished in the 1960s. Numerous designs by him for garden architecture and ornaments survive, but, apart from a few designs for plinths for statues, none are for executed projects; according to the Baron the landscape consultant was a rather obscure Parisian, Elie Lainé.

Architect and contractors

Baron Ferdinand described Destailleur as *...a purist in style, painstaking, conscientious, and of the most scrupulous honesty. During the eighteen years of my relations with him there was never the smallest difference between us. But he was dilatory and unpractical. He had not the faintest conception of the needs of a large establishment, sacrificed the most urgent household requirements to external architectural features, and had the most supreme contempt for light, air and all internal conveniences... .* (11)

On the other hand, he had unqualified admiration for his contractor, Edward Conder, of the firm of Edward Conder and Son, of Kingsland Road in London: *...my builder, Mr. Conder,*

Above: It was intended that the Manor look like a sixteenth century house but built with the most modern techniques including cast iron girders.

Above left: The brick construction was clad in elaborately carved Bath stone.

Below left and right: The reshaping of the hill before the construction work of the Manor began required substantial earthworks which were carried out by manpower and horses.

Chandeliers inspired by eighteenth century models, were bought in Paris by Baron Ferdinand and electrified, around 1890, for use at Waddesdon.

than whom I have never met a more trustworthy business man... . The whole amazing evocation of Blois, Chambord and other châteaux on a Buckinghamshire hilltop, the house's eighteenth century interiors with their fabulous contents, were solidly backed up by late Victorian technology. Destailleur had nothing to do with this, and the executive English architect, Edward H. Burnell, probably very little; it was Conder who master-minded it.

Reshaping, materials and building

The Victorian railway system allowed materials to be collected from all over England, but the building site at Waddesdon was two miles from the nearest railway line, and on treacherous sandy soil above clay at the top of a steep gradient. A Waddesdon siding was formed next to Quainton Road railway station. From there materials were transferred closer to the bottom of the hill on the private steam tramway built a few years previously by the Duke of Buckingham to convey goods to his house at Wotton. The final stage up to the hill top and to the huge builder's yard shown in surviving photographs was by a steam-powered cable railway. The site itself, the garden terraces and the road, had to be levelled or landscaped by manual labour. Gangs of navvies were employed on this, supplemented by a hundred or so local workmen under the burly Mr. Sims who, as Bailiff to the Estate, was to be a dominant figure at Waddesdon for nearly fifty years and to cause some local comment by leaving a small fortune when he died. What especially caught contemporary imagination were the hundreds of full-grown trees, some from as far afield as Kent, which were hauled through the local towns and villages by teams of twelve to sixteen Percheron mares imported from Normandy and were planted on the bare hillside, though not always with success.

The house was built of brick, but entirely faced with Bath stone. Above the plaster ceilings was a complicated wrought iron structure, with big main beams supporting secondary beams which in turn supported timber floor joists. In a domestic context it was an

A view of the Aviary from the coloured diascope photographs commissioned by Miss Alice, around 1910.

advanced use of metal beams to cover wide spans and enabled the plan of the upper floor to differ from that of the floor below; in the West Wing, for instance, the partition walls of a series of smaller rooms are perched on the wrought iron beams above the enormous morning room.

In addition to a plethora of open coal fires the house was centrally heated throughout, the height of luxury at the time, by means of grilles in the floors on the ground and first floors and radiators on the top floor. It was originally lit by gas made in the Estate's own gasworks at Westcott; but electricity generated on the Estate was installed in the new Morning Room Wing in 1889-90, and the rest of the house was converted to it in the next few years. The electrical engineer employed was E.T. Mackrill of Aylesbury, who worked for other Rothschilds in Buckinghamshire and London, and made ...*a leading speciality of the newest and most artistic ideas on the electric lighting of houses and mansions... .* His fittings and bulbs for chandeliers disguised as wax candles feature in the first photographs, and were admired by Queen Victoria when she visited Waddesdon in 1890.

The costs

What did it all cost? In spite of the loss of building accounts and correspondence, some idea can be obtained from entries in Baron Ferdinand's bank account at N.M. Rothschild and Sons in London. Conder was paid £224,855 between 1877 and 1894, a sum which can be conjecturally broken down, on the basis of the dates of the payments, as made up of about £160,000 for the main house, £40,000 for stables, aviary and garden works, and £25,000 for the West Wing and other additions made in 1889-91. Burnell received £3,028 in 1877-81, and Mackrill £6,914 in 1888-98; payments made in Paris by Rothschild Frères, recorded only to July 1879, amount to £7,332 for Destailleur and £554 for Lainé. All this is exclusive of what was paid from the Baron's local account with the London and County Bank, Aylesbury. This probably includes payments for the ground works and approach roads, which the Baron's solicitor James James told a friend cost £55,000; possibly for the glasshouses; and certainly for the numerous houses and estate buildings erected by the Baron in the villages or elsewhere on the property. At the same period Windmill Hill Farm with its farm dwelling, part of the Waddesdon estate, produced a rental of £770 per year.(12)

The eighteenth century lean-to *secretaire* in the West Gallery is arranged with the same objects on display as in Miss Alice's time. All the fine Sèvres porcelain pieces come from the collections of Baron Ferdinand and Miss Alice.

The bank account also gives some idea of the cost of the contents. There are payments to London dealers such as Colnaghi, Durlacher and Quaritch, but they only amount to a few thousand; by far the biggest total was to the Bond Street firm of Wertheimer: £132,536 in all between 1879 and 1897. There is no identifiable record of what was paid for 'curiosities' and panelling on the Continent, especially in Paris.

All in all, Baron Ferdinand's capital expenditure on Waddesdon, exclusive of land purchase, must have been in excess of half a million pounds. In contemporary terms this was an enormous outlay, and made Waddesdon one of the half dozen or so most expensive country-house projects of the Victorian age in England. According to the Baron's notebooks his income in the late 1880s, when most of his capital expenditure was finished with, was about £80,000 a year. This was a very large late-Victorian income - not as large as the Duke of Devonshire's £180,000 or the Duke of Buccleuch's £217,000, but such great magnates had to support half a dozen or so country houses and a string of children, siblings and dowagers; the Baron, with no dependents and only one country house, could lavish money on Waddesdon and give generously to charity as well.

Chapter 4

LIFE AT WADDESDON

Previous page: The Dining Room at Waddesdon. The room is furnished today as it is seen in photographs from the time of Baron Ferdinand.

Left: A watercolour dated 1871, by the fashionable artist John Frederick Tayler, showing Baron Ferdinand hunting in Buckinghamshire.

Waddesdon was built for large-scale entertaining, but of a specialised nature. It was designed for the huge house-parties which were a feature of late Victorian England, and were made possible by the growing railway network which enabled tired politicians, or socialites taking part in the Season in London, to retreat for a few days from the summer heat of Mayfair or Westminster to the coolness of the country. Such parties proliferated, but Waddesdon was one of a dozen or so houses which set the pace and the tone through their size, the quality of entertainment which they provided, and the people who came to them.

House parties

There were the small autumn house-parties at Waddesdon, for the shooting or the hunting, but these did not play an important part in the life of the House. Baron Ferdinand was sometimes there on his own, or with a few relatives or friends, especially around Christmas. For large portions of the year, when he was away in London, abroad, or in other country houses, the great rooms stood empty. The House only really came into its own half a dozen or so times a year when, with his sister Alice as hostess, he gave his renowned 'Saturday to Monday' house-parties. These took place in May, June or July, usually for between twenty and thirty people.

The occasional writer, artist or museum director came to stay: Guy de Maupassant and Lord Leighton once, Henry James and Mrs. Humphrey Ward several times. But such people form an insignificant element in the visitors' book. Although Waddesdon dealt in the best, in house-party terms this meant not the intellectual or artistic, but the social and political best - summed-up in the one word 'Society'. The thousand or so aristocrats, politicians, lawyers, courtiers, diplomats and their wives, who concentrated in themselves most of the power, wealth, lineage or glamour of late Victorian England, were luxury goods as labour-intensive and exquisite as the Baron's French furniture.

Society

Three main groups from society can be separated out from the Waddesdon visitors' book. The first was made up of the Prince of Wales - the future Edward VII - and his circle. As Queen Victoria lived in semi-retirement, the Prince was the acknowledged leader of society, and the fact that the Rothschilds were his friends, and had mastered the difficult art of keeping him amused, was the main reason for their success not just in gaining an entry to Society but in playing a dominant part in it. He stayed at Waddesdon fourteen times in all, including one unfortunate time in 1897 when he slipped on the West Staircase on his way down to breakfast and fractured his knee-cap.

The Souls

The second group were the Souls. This was the nickname given to a group of fifty or so lively and intelligent upper-class men and women - including A.J.Balfour, George Nathaniel Curzon and Margot Asquith - who made something of a stir in the 1880s and 90s by setting themselves up in opposition to what they considered the Philistine materialism of the Prince of Wales and his circle. It was a measure of Baron Ferdinand's tolerance and

This charming, naive watercolour was painted in 1885 by Mademoiselle Cécile Hofer, a lifelong friend of Miss Alice, who frequently came to visit her at Waddesdon.

gifts as a host and a friend that he was accepted by both the Souls and the Marlborough House set as one of themselves, and he entertained members of both groups at Waddesdon, often in the same house-parties.

Politicians

The third group, overlapping with the other two, was political. Baron Ferdinand succeeded his cousin Nathaniel as Liberal M.P. for Aylesbury in 1885. Gladstone came to stay at Waddesdon in 1886 but, like many other Liberals, the Baron could not accept Irish

Fancy dress parties were popular in the Victorian period. Here Baron Ferdinand is shown in the sixteenth century costume of a German nobleman.

Home Rule; he seceded from the main party in or soon after 1886, and became a Liberal Unionist. He seldom spoke in the House of Commons; his political influence was behind the scenes. Summer house-parties, while Par-liament was in session, provided a useful ambience in which politicians could meet each other to discuss issues, plan campaigns or cement alliances. Waddesdon played an important, if impalpable, role in bringing Liberal Unionists together with Conservatives. Liberals, like Lord Hartington and Joseph Chamberlain, met there with Conservatives such as Balfour and Lord Randolph Churchill, and after a game of tennis, cricket or a convivial dinner could stroll in the gardens or retire to the Smoking Room, to cement relationships which were to lead to the Conservatives joining with dissenting Liberals in the Unionist Party, the ancestor of modern Conservatism.

Entertainment at Waddesdon

Several weeks' work must have preceded the moment on a series of summer mornings when the carriages and horses deposited the first guests beneath the port-cochère at Waddesdon. Old photographs show how the wealth of the hothouses was drawn on to fill the great bowls in the main rooms with palms and exotic plants, to bank up more flowers in the conservatory, and cover the Dining Room table with elaborate floral arrangements - all the work of a specialist member of the garden staff known as the decorator. One of the lawns on the entrance front of the House was invariably set out for tennis and a striped marquee set up by the court, for tea and shade. There were two more little marquees on the garden terrace. Down in the stables a string of elegant pony traps, drawn by black ponies and driven by liveried grooms, were ready to convey guests anywhere in village, park or grounds. The lawns had been freshly mown by the three mowing machines, each drawn by a pony wearing leather boots to protect the turf. The fountains played. The great terrace to the south of the house was ablaze with flowers. Not a flower or leaf was allowed to be out of place. Lady Warwick related how she came to the house-warming at Waddesdon on a stormy day when the rain had battered the flower beds to pieces: *...I happened to be awake at five o'clock on the Sunday morning ... I went to the window to discover whether it was wet or fine, and a truly amazing sight met my eyes. I saw an army of gardeners at work,* *taking out the damaged plants and putting in new ones. ...After breakfast I went into the grounds... . The gardeners had vanished. ...Not a damaged plant was to be seen anywhere... .*

Entertainments at Waddesdon included tennis, followed by tea on the lawn and a short walk round the grounds or the house, to look at the contents of the latter or visit the Aviary and the Menagerie. Guests could walk down the hill to the great Conservatory and the Dairy by way of the rock garden, admire the exotic plants in the former and the collection of majolica and other 'curiosities' on display in the latter, be given refreshments in the Dairy. They could also make a visit to the model farm and emerge to find a string of pony-carriages waiting to carry them back up the hill to the house. A regular house-party feature was an outing in carriages down through the three miles of parkland to lunch at Miss Alice's pavilion at Eythrope, a tour of the garden there and, if the weather was suitable, a trip by launch to take tea at a summer-house a mile or so up the river.

On special occasions, such as the opening house-party or a royal visit, there were firework displays arranged by Brocks, the famous firework makers from Crystal Palace, followed by a ball. A band or orchestra was

One of Baron Ferdinand's tea parties on the North Lawn in front of the Manor. Marquees were set up and wicker garden furniture was put out on the lawn.

often brought down from London, to play in the Conservatory during dinner.

The Shah of Persia, who came for the night in July 1889, was entertained by a torch-light procession, a conjuring show, and a display of tricks by the Baron's poodle, Emperor Frederich III, who came once. Queen Victoria came for the day on 14th May 1889. Her visit was something of a triumph, because she went out comparative-ly little, and on the whole disapproved of her son's friends, but she had heard so much about Waddesdon that she came there at her

For parties in the summer the east side of the lawn was laid out as a tennis court. The photograph shows the Prince of Wales playing tennis at Waddesdon.

Poupon: *...Nothing pleased the Shah half so much as Mr. Charles Bertram's conjuring, and he shrieked with laughter as the able prestidigitator extracted eggs from the nose of the Persian Grand Vizier and produced half-crowns from the Imperial ears... . (13)*

Other royal visitors, apart from the Prince of Wales, included his two sons, Princes Eddy and George, who came frequently, King Leopold of the Belgians and the German

own request and thoroughly enjoyed her visit.

Different visitors had different reactions. Sir Algernon West said that his only criticism of Waddesdon and Eythrope was that they were too perfect; and one can see how, in that magnificent and childless house, guests may occasionally have longed for a little disorder. Henry James spent five days at Waddesdon in August 1885, and wrote to his friend,

A photograph, taken about 1910, of the now demolished glass houses. The terracotta figures which date from the nineteenth century are now at Eythrope.

Grace Norton: *...the gilded bondage of that gorgeous place will last me a long time...* . This did not stop him returning five more times. Lady Battersea was a frequent visitor, and from her diaries one gets the impression, not surprisingly, that some house-parties came off better than others.(14) The distinctive quality of Waddesdon at its best, as described by her and others, seems to have been a combination of splendour, comfort, and informality. Guests were never regimented, and the great set-pieces were interspersed with pleasant lazy conversations in shady corners of the garden, in the Smoking Room, or sitting out on the terrace after dinner in the long summer twilight - just as the French furniture was interspersed with the comfortably upholstered sofas and leather armchairs which feature prominently in old photographs, although most of them were weeded out once the house was opened to the public in June 1959.

The plan of the House

The plan of the house can be read in terms of the house-parties for which it was created. The guests needed somewhere to congregate in the day-time, and more formally, in the evening. The two Drawing-Rooms were the formal rooms. Guests would have assembled before dinner in the Grey Drawing Room. From there there was a convenient way through the Red Drawing Room to the Dining Room, but Victorians liked to make something of a procession of the move, couple by couple, to the Dining Room, and it is possible that a longer and more formal route may have been preferred, by way of the West Gallery, the Oval Hall, the East Gallery, and the Conservatory. After dinner one of the Drawing Rooms would have been set out with card tables for bridge; the men, if they wished, could retreat to the Smoking Room and the Billiard Room in the Bachelors' Wing.

A deficiency of the original plan, in its cut-down form, was that the West Gallery had to serve as the general day-time living room; it was too small, and the Baron could only get in and out of his own rooms by going through it. The Morning Room was built to take its place and the Baron then moved his bedroom suite to the floor above it. Previously it had been above the two rooms he used himself, the Green Sitting Room and the tower room, with private access by means of a little newel staircase running

Before the age of motorisation the lawn mowers were pulled by ponies which wore leather boots in order to protect the turf. This picture was taken on the cricket field in front of the cricket pavilion.

from the Green Sitting Room up to his bedroom, and on to the top floor.

Miss Alice's sitting-room and bedroom were located over the Dining Room. Above the Grey Drawing Room and the Small Library was the State Apartment, made up of Dressing-Room, Bedroom, and the Green Boudoir, with its splendid eighteenth-century panelling. Here the Prince of Wales, the Shah and other royalties were installed, and Queen Victoria rested after luncheon. She was presented with a jewelled fan by Baron Ferdinand, kneeling like an Elizabethan courtier in the Green Boudoir.

There were further sets of bedrooms and dressing-rooms for married couples on the first floor, single bedrooms in the Bachelors'

Wing, and further guest bedrooms, if needed, on the second floor.

Staff and servants

The perfection of Waddesdon depended on its servants. There were around thirty-one indoor staff in the time of Baron Ferdinand and Miss Alice: a house steward or head butler, an under-butler, four footmen and the Baron's valet, an electric-light man, two odd men (one of them known in Miss Alice's time as 'Dripping', because he sold dripping at a special rate to anyone on the Estate who called in for it), and a Steward's Room boy; a head housekeeper, an assistant housekeeper, a Still-Room maid and nine housemaids; a chef (in the Baron's time, M. Bonner, who previously had been chef to the Tsar), an assistant chef, a confectioner, a woman cook,

The west side of the Dairy as it is today. The building was used as a dairy until the late 1980s and was restored in recent years for use as offices and a hospitality centre.

and four scullery and kitchen maids. In addition, a laundryman and four laundry-maids worked in the separate Laundry building down the hill, but probably ate in the Servants' Hall; there were two caretakers, and a policeman, on loan from the Buckinghamshire Constabulary, acted as a night-watchman. The footmen, the chefs, and the confectioner moved to and fro between Waddesdon and London, but the rest of the staff were permanently resident at Waddesdon.

The Kitchen (today the Tea Rooms) was not

The water garden was restored and replanted to its original appearance. Its rock formations and bridges are reminiscent of landscape gardens of the pre-Romantic period.

originally open to the forecourt, as it is now, but shut off by a wall and planting. Entry to the service quarters was by way of a back drive leading to the east end of the Bachelors' Wing, and through an archway into a glass-roofed courtyard; from the courtyard a wide service corridor led to the main service staircase in the big north-east tower, where there was a hand-operated luggage lift, later to be replaced by an electric goods lift. The Still-Room, the Steward's Room (where upper servants ate, waited on by the fourth footman and the Steward's Room boy), the Housekeeper's Room, the Kitchen and Servants' Hall and ancillary rooms were grouped around the courtyard and corridor. A ramp by the back entrance led down through a tunnel to the basement; carts could drive down it, and right on through the basement by way of a broad corridor, to make

deliveries. The basement contained Vegetable Larders and Butchers' Rooms under the Kitchen and in the main block, Flower, Lamp, Battery and Boiler Rooms, Cellars, a Butler's Pantry under the Breakfast Room, and a Carpenter's Shop under the West Hall.

Male servants slept in the Bachelors' Wing, and female servants were segregated from them on the top floor of the main block, where there were also two Linen-Rooms, looking north and south, under the central dome. Visitors' maids were neatly catered for in eight little rooms, one above the other in pairs off two staircases across the main bedroom corridor from their employers' rooms, and half their height.

Influence of the Manor

Waddesdon was more than life at the Manor - or 'on the hill' as the locals put it. The house staff made up only a small proportion of the employees on the estate. Insurance records for 1904 show 346 employees at Waddesdon, including farm workers but exclusive of house staff, and 71 at Eythrope. Those at Waddesdon included about 150 in the gardens, 25 in the stables, twelve building and repair staff, four *...attending woodworking machines and saws worked by power...*, two at the Westcott gasworks, four blacksmiths and three *...steam roller, steam threshing machine and traction engine men... .* The bulk of this workforce lived in

Waddesdon village and went back there for their midday meal so that, as Aubrey Hicks, a Waddesdon boy, remembered it, *...at meal times and knocking-off time it was like an army coming down the High Street... .* (15)

for the use of the villagers and supplied with a pavilion and a resident professional; but what especially caught local imagination, and entered local legend in rather the same way as the Percheron mares and their waggonloads of trees, was the annual 'Baron's Treat'. This was given on a Thursday at the end of July or beginning of August. Probably more than two thousand people came, for everyone on the Estate, of all ages, was invited. The park and gardens, which were normally closed to the public, were thrown open for them; children marched down the High Street behind the village's two brass bands

Rothschild munificence flowed down the hill. Waddesdon, like the other Rothschild villages and estates, was regarded with envy by its neighbours, especially in the lean years of the agricultural depression in the 1880s and 90s when most landlords had little to spare for their tenants. Cottages, a school, a club and a village hall were built, water and gas laid, a cricket field laid out

Above: The wrought ironwork which adorns many buildings on the Estate is mainly of German origin and dates from the eighteenth century.

Right: The Curio Room at the Dairy, decorated with antlers, faiences and other curiosities.

to the field next to the cricket field, on which were stalls, swings and roundabouts and also an enormous marquee, in which a lavish tea was served to everyone in two sittings; at some stage the Baron and his current house-party drove down the hill and were greeted with appropriate cheers.

The Estate had its own distinctive architecture, quite apart from the French fantasies up the hill. Home Farm, Dairy, Estate Office, Lodges, Cricket Pavilion, the 'Five Arrows', the Institute and houses in the village and the Stables at Eythrope were all, or nearly all, designed by W.F. Taylor, an Aylesbury architect, who evolved his own distinctive version of what was called at the time the 'Old English' style, rich with half-timbering, verandahs, high roofs, elaborately patterned chimneystacks or tile-hanging, and occasional charming panels of terracotta detail.

Above: Aylesbury station decorated with flags and festoons for the arrival of Queen Victoria who visited Waddesdon village and the Manor on May 8th, 1890.

Right: Extract from a poem by Henry James, written on one of his visits to Waddesdon, in the *Livre d'Or*:

Baron, I never turned a rhyme,
  I only handle prose;
I haven't metre, tune or time,
  As everybody knows.
And yet in this exalted place,
  Amid a choir seraphic,
I rashly do attempt to trace,
  A tribute autographic!

Opposite: Miss Alice, until her old age, used to walk her dogs in the gardens at Waddesdon and Eythrope.

Chapter 5

MISS ALICE
DE ROTHSCHILD

Baron Ferdinand died of a stroke in his bath at Waddesdon on 18th December 1898, the day before his fifty ninth birthday. He left Waddesdon and his London house to his sister Alice. She was born in 1847, the youngest of the family. Photographs of her as a girl and young woman show her with a broad brow, firm full lips and a strong chin, not conventionally pretty, but full of character and, to twentieth century eyes at least, by no means unattractive. But such looks were not admired in the 1860s. *...The poor girl...*, her aunt Charlotte wrote in November 1866, *...is a real shuttle-cock, flung from the home of a compassionate relative, under the roof of some other commiserating friend - and all this flying, travelling, rushing, hurrying... because she has no*

mother to love her - because she has an ugly face and no husband to fall in love with her... .

The formidable Miss Alice

Two events helped change *'the poor girl'* to the formidable 'Miss Alice' of later years. After her sister-in-law died in 1866, she acted as hostess for her brother Ferdinand, first at Leighton House and then at Waddesdon. The death of her father in 1874 made her a rich woman, for he left her a considerable fortune including (to the surprise of her relatives) the original Rothschild family home in Frankfurt and a house and estate at the Grüneburg, outside it. She sold the Frankfurt

property almost immediately to her brother-in-law Baron Willy de Rothschild, bought the Eyth-rope estate in 1875, No. 142 Piccadilly, next to her brother's house, in 1886, and a property at Grasse, in the South of France, in 1888. She bought the Grasse property as a winter home, for she suffered intermittently from rheumatic fever. She built what became known as the Villa Victoria on it - in honour, and with the permission of, Queen Victoria whom she frequently entertained there.

For similar reasons of health she never slept at Eythrope, where the damp river air was thought to be bad for her. The house on the

Left: Textiles are an important part of the Collection at Waddesdon. The State Bedroom contains silk curtains and bedhangings specially woven for Waddesdon, by the silk weaving firms of Lyon.

Below: This French eighteenth century snuffbox was painted in the Sèvres porcelain factory for Madame de Pompadour. It shows her favourite pet dogs Inès and Mimi.

property had been demolished before her time; she built a relatively modest pavilion, to the designs of George Devey, for meals and entertainment only.

...Gifted with a manly intellect and a firm sense of duty..., her cousin Lady Battersea wrote of her after her death, *....also an unusually strong power of will and inflexibility of purpose, she pursued her way of life, carrying out her improvements, managing her property, looking after every detail of her estate, undeterred by any opposition that she might meet with... .* This is polite obituary language to describe an alarming woman. Whether or not the story is true that she ordered Queen Victoria to get off one of her flower-beds, the Queen certainly referred to her with admiration as the 'all-powerful'.

Lady Battersea describes her directing operations at Grasse *...in the voice, and with the manner, of a Napoleon... .* At Waddesdon she drove herself everywhere in a little two-pony chaise, always wearing the same soft grey clothes and a panama hat. Nothing escaped her. Aubrey Hicks, who was a garden boy there just before the 1914-18 War, describes how *...Miss Alice de Rothschild,*

Once a year, in the summer, Baron Ferdinand gave a garden tea party to the staff and villagers of Waddesdon and Upper Winchendon, which was popularly known as the Baron's Treat. Marquees were set up on the lawns, an orchestra played and tea and soft drinks were served.

when walking round the grounds, always carried a silver paddle to dig out anything that offended her, and Mr. George Staunton, in his uniform of brown velvet coat and twill breeches and leggings followed in the rear picking up the rubbish. On these occasions the working people had to hide in the plantation until the Lady of the Manor had passed by... . (16)

Remote and alarming though she could seem to her tenants and employees, she worked hard to improve their health and education, provided free medical assistance, installed drainage, built cottages, a second school and an institute in the village, and knew much

more about individuals on the estate than they may have realised, as her surviving letters to Mr. Johnson, the Head Gardener at Waddesdon, make clear.

These all start, typically enough, with a peremptory *'Johnson...'*, but the dominant impression they leave is of a humane, humorous, decisive and intelligent woman. *...Quality...*, she wrote to him, *...is the one thing you must study in all your work at Waddesdon...* . What the son of her Head Gardener at Grasse has called *...her methodical, minute and almost manic pursuit of perfection...* may have been uncomfortable for any gardener who was in the offing when

she found a weed in a flower-bed, or for the cucumbers grown through tubes to make sure that they all came out an identical shape; but its legacy was what became known as 'the Waddesdon

Above: The helmet of the emperor Charles V is one of the major contributions Miss Alice made to the Armoury Corridor after the Waddesdon Bequest, her brother's collection, went to the British Museum in 1898. The Armoury Corridor is part of the Bachelor's Wing which has recently been restored.

Left: The rhinoceros inspired by the well known engraving by Dürer. It came from the Grüneburg, the family house outside Frankfurt, where it had been a garden ornament.

Right: An ivory vase from the private collection of the King of France, Louis XVI. Ivory turning was the favourite pastime of royalty all over Europe. This vase is decorated with the most elaborate jewel-like gilt bronze mounts. Very few objects of this quality survive today.

Miss Alice hunting in the English countryside. A watercolour, 1870, by John Frederick Tayler, an artist whose work was greatly appreciated by Victorian society.

standard', the rigorously high criteria of care and maintenance which still reign in the house today, and are responsible for the superb condition of its contents.

A careful collector

She added to the collections of Waddesdon with discrimination, especially in order to fill the gap left by her brother's bequest to the British Museum. She continued to give large house-parties, although not quite so large as her brother's. But entries in the visitors' book cease after 1915, never to be resumed in her lifetime, for by the end of the 1914-18 War she was an invalid. During the War her young English cousin Evelyn de Rothschild, whom she had intended to be her heir, was killed on the Western Front; and when she died in May 1922 she was found to have left Waddesdon and Eythrope, without forewarning, to James de Rothschild, son of Edmond de Rothschild of Paris.

Above: This small picture is one of Miss Alice's finest acquisitions. *The Judgement of Paris,* a painting by the Dutch Mannerist artist Joachim Antonisz Wtewael is now on display in the Smoking Room in the Bachelors' Wing.

Left: This curious *objet d'art* is one of a pair made from Japanese lacquer vases elaborately mounted in Paris. The motif of snakes holding the vase is also found in objects from Queen Marie-Antoinette's collection of the 1780s. Baron Ferdinand kept these vases in the Tower Room.

Opposite: James and Dorothy de Rothschild inherited Waddesdon in 1922 and bequeathed it to the National Trust in 1957. Green damask woven for the Baron's Room forms the background of this photograph.

Chapter 6

JAMES AND DOROTHY
DE ROTHSCHILD

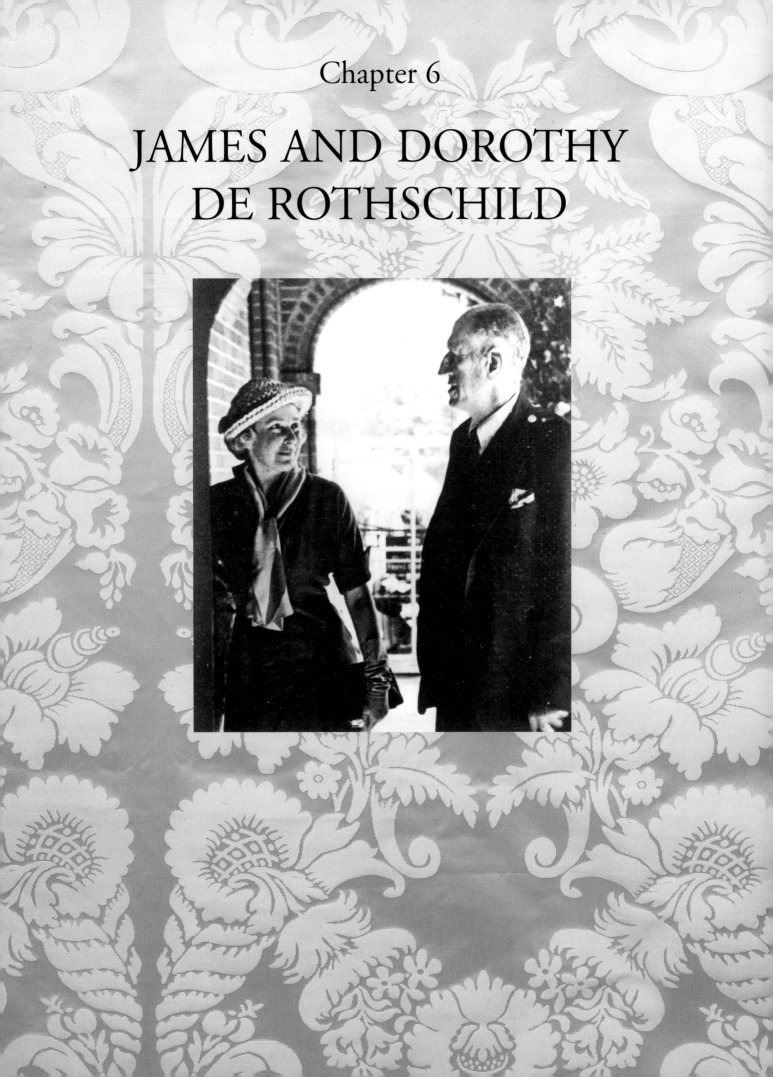

James de Rothschild was physically the most distinctive of the owners of Waddesdon. His tall, willowy frame surmounted by a massive, battered but curiously attractive head was a gift to caricaturists on the English race-courses and in the House of Commons, and reflected his idiosyncratic charm and picaresque and unusual early career.

He had gone from a French Lycée to Trinity College in Cambridge, rode and hunted with abandon, briefly took time off from horses to win the Harkness Prize at the University for a Shakespearean essay, absconded to Australia for eighteen months to escape a career in the Paris bank, was run to earth working as a cattle-hand, reconciled with his parents and finally went into the bank after a year's travel round the world.

In 1914 he joined the French Army in the ranks, was attached to the British Army as an interpreter; buried under an upturned lorry, and disinterred by a passing British officer ('My God! It's Jimmy Rothschild! Dig him up!' he exclaimed, as he poked the mud off his face with the toe of his boot). The accident left him physically shattered, and although he recovered sufficiently to raise a Jewish battalion under Allenby in Palestine in 1918, and retained his infectious interest in every-

Below: This painting by Paul Benney shows the proposed model for the new Supreme Court Building in Jerusalem with those involved in the project, including Lord Rothschild, the Israeli Prime Minister Yitzhak Rabin and the Foreign Minister Shimon Perez. The building was financed by the Yad Hanadiv Foundation, established and chaired by Dorothy de Rothschild, and was inaugurated in 1992.

thing that came his way, he never fully regained his health or strength; nor were matters improved when a stray golf ball hit by the Duc de Gramont removed his right eye on the golf course at Deauville - to be replaced by a glass eye with a monocle stylishly inserted in front of it.

Political and philanthropic interests

James de Rothschild's father was one of the founders of Zionism and a major pioneer of Jewish settlement in Palestine, and he him-

Above: Hannah Mathilde was Miss Alice's sister, better known as Baroness Willy. She is shown here in a photograph taken after 1898 with the portrait of Perdita by Gainsborough in the background.

Oval: Thomas Gainsborough's portrait of Mrs. Mary Robinson, the famous actress popularly known as Perdita, who won the affection of the Prince Regent.

Left: The series of decorative panels illustrating the fairy tale of the Sleeping Beauty was painted by Leon Bakst for the dining room of James and Dorothy de Rothschild's town house.

Opposite right: Detail of the exquisite ormolu mounts of the table which the cabinet maker Riesener made in 1787 for Queen Marie-Antoinette's apartments in the Petit Trianon at Versailles, and which was sold during the French Revolution. Baron Ferdinand bought it in 1882 at the Hamilton Palace Sale and placed it in the Tower Room, where it can be seen today.

self worked for the same causes with dedicated enthusiasm. At home he was an active Liberal, M.P. for Ely from 1929 to 1945, and an important and popular figure in the racing world. The two interests found expression at Waddesdon in the thoroughbred stud which he built on the estate, and the Liberal rallies held on the cricket pitch, where Lloyd George and other politicians spoke to the crowds from the pavilion roof.

When his father died in 1934 he inherited a share of his collection; this, combined with his inheritance from Miss Alice, left him little scope or incentive to add to the collections at Waddesdon. However, he and his wife Dorothy worked to bring it into the post-Great War world; the house was rewired and put on the mains, extra bathrooms and a service lift were installed, inside and outside staff reduced and much work contracted out, so that the Estate ceased to be as much a little world on its own as it had been in the days of Baron Ferdinand and Miss Alice.

Their main essay in artistic patronage was in London. In 1913, while still unmarried, James had commissioned the Russian artist Leon Bakst to paint a series of murals for the drawing room of his house in Park Street. These were completed in 1922, when he installed them in the dining room of another house, in St James' Place, into which he and his wife had moved on his marriage after the war. Their subject is the Sleeping Beauty, but at his suggestion his family and friends were portrayed as characters in the story.

In the 1939-45 War (in which he served in the Ministry of Supply) he and his wife moved into the Bachelors' Wing, peat replaced coal in the grates, the roses in the rose garden gave way to tomatoes and the main part of the house was given over to a hundred or so under-five evacuees - a rather touching interlude in the history of a house so curiously childless throughout the rest of its time in private ownership. When he died in 1957, he left Waddesdon Manor, the contents of the main rooms, 120 acres around it, and a large endowment to the National Trust. The rest of the estate was left to his wife, who enlarged Eythrope and lived there until she died in 1988. The relationship between Waddesdon and the Rothschilds remains a very close one, and the costs are met, in the main, by Rothschild trusts.

Dorothy de Rothschild, disciple and admirer of Miss Alice

Dorothy de Rothschild was born Dorothy Pinto, and married when she was only seventeen. She came to Waddesdon in 1922 and, as she became Chairman of the Management Committee which was set up under the National Trust, her connection with the house lasted sixty-six years, longer than that of any other member of the family. It was with her guidance and support that the house was opened to the public, and the great series of catalogues of the collections, which is still in production, began to be assembled.

Her pride and interest in Waddesdon were without end, and her knowledge of the house, its contents and the methods of conserving them, never stopped growing.

Garnitures of vases in Chinese porcelain, fine sculpture, the best of English eighteenth century portraiture and authentic textile furnishings combine to form the specific character of Rothschild opulence, which Waddesdon allows a unique opportunity to appreciate.

she had to do so. ...*She never said a nasty thing about anyone. If you were in trouble she always produced the person you needed....* She was compulsively tidy; a guest remembers her running out with a broom to sweep away leaves which had collected beneath a car parked in front of the house.

She set up, largely financed and served as chairwoman of the Yad Hanadiv Foundation, maintaining the commitment to social and religious institutions in Palestine, and later Israel, which had been established by her father-in-law and continued by her husband. She was active in other Jewish charities in London, was Deputy County Organiser of the Women's Voluntary Service in Buckinghamshire, and sat for many years on the Buckinghamshire County Council.

She was a disciple and admirer of Miss Alice, demanding and expecting prompt service and high criteria, but was a more approachable person, humorous and wise, and an unending source of support and good advice to those who asked for it.

Her niece Anne Marks vividly remembers her distinctive personality: ...*a sort of shyness..., combined with great strength of character and a complete lack of ostentation. If she wore pearls, they were tucked into her clothes; she never wore furs or make-up. She had ...wonderful soft white skin, very rosy cheeks and very black eyes...* . She loved people and racing, but never went to grand parties if she could help it, disliked entertaining on a large scale, and was always in a slight state when

One of her and her husband's most attractive ventures was to give refuge at Waddesdon to boys from the Flerscheim-Sichel Institute, a Jewish school in Frankfurt, who they got out from Germany to England just in time before the 1939-45 war. They occupied a house in the village called the Cedars, and former Cedars Boys still come back to visit from time to time; Mrs de Rothschild presided over a reunion dinner in 1983 and in 1993 the survivors erected a plaque recording their gratitude on the Red Lion Steps in the gardens at Waddesdon.

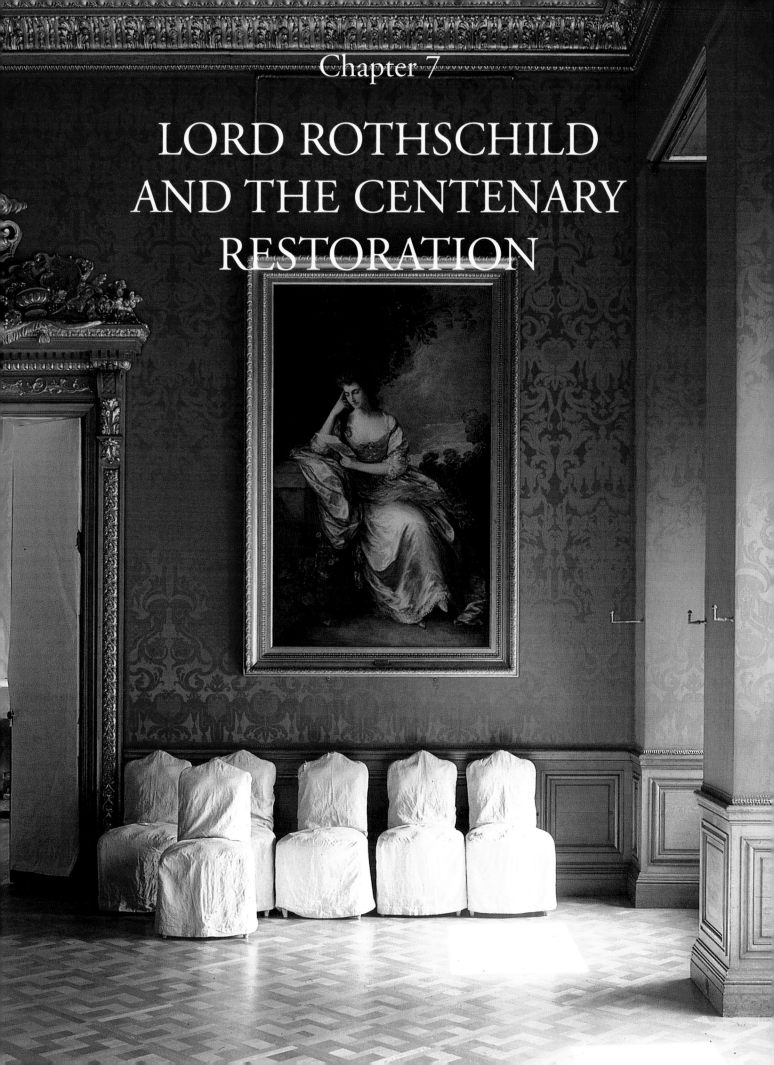

Chapter 7

LORD ROTHSCHILD AND THE CENTENARY RESTORATION

Previous page: Each autumn, after the closure of the Manor to the public, all the furniture is covered with loose covers to protect the fabrics from dust and light.

Left: The elephant automaton was made in London by the French clockmaker H. Martinet. It plays a tune, the elephant moves its ears, eyes, trunk and tail; the figures and animals on the base also move.

Below: During the centenary restoration the elephant automaton was dismantled and conserved. Its mechanism is now in good working order and once a week it is demonstrated to the public.

Programme of restoration

In contemplating what was to happen in the succeeding years one has a strong feeling of a pattern repeating itself, as to celebrate the House's centenary a major programme of restoration, re-arrangement

Mrs. James de Rothschild died in December 1988. She left the bulk of her very large fortune, including Eythrope and those parts of the Waddesdon estate which had not been given to the National Trust, to her husband's cousin Jacob Rothschild, who was to succeed his father Victor as 4th Baron Rothschild in 1990. He is one of the English Rothschilds; his great-uncle, the second Baron, founded the Tring Zoological Museum at his house in Hertfordshire, and used to drive himself around in a carriage pulled by four zebras. Jacob Rothschild had been a member of the National Trust's Management Committee at Waddesdon for a number of years, and he now succeeded Mrs. de Rothschild as its Chairman.

and refurbishment was embarked upon. Waddesdon Manor vanished behind scaffolding and was closed to the public for three and a half years. Three miles of copper pipe and twelve miles of electric cable were used to rewire the house and to replace the plumbing and heating systems. Much of the stonework and all the leadwork on the roof was renewed. The contents were put into store or removed for repair; thousands of pieces of porcelain disappeared into boxes lined with chamois leather. Furniture, pictures and

Lord Rothschild
who steered
the centenary
restoration from
1988.

delicate objects were boxed up or sheathed in tissue paper and dust covers, internal wall surfaces were covered with fire-retardant paper and every floor was taken up. At the peak there were fifty artisans working on the house, and more in the workshops which were established in the stables for the repair and conservation of fabrics and the seventy pairs of curtains made from silks woven for Baron Ferdinand in the 1870s. Two new suites were formed in parts of the first floor which had been substantially altered in the 1960s; the cellars were in part rearranged and opened to the public; the great parterre and its fountain were restored; bulldozers dug out the silted-up water garden; the Dairy was added to and internally remodelled.

The architects, consultants and the staff, Peter Inskip as architect, Rosamund Griffin as Keeper of the Collection, Antony Morgan, as building manager, aided by a small army of

The Red Drawing Room. In 1994 Waddesdon won an award for its light fittings and non-intrusive picture lighting, which was developed specially for the house.

sense of style, his low threshold of boredom, and his obsessive interest in detail (...*all life is ninety-five percent detail, five percent inspiration...*, as he puts it). Common to both of them, as to all Rothschilds, or at least all Rothschilds who have had anything to do with Waddesdon, is the conviction that only the best is good enough.

There the similarities end, however. Waddesdon in the 1990s was being restored for different purposes, in a different world, and under a different type of ownership. The melancholy, withdrawn Baron Ferdinand played almost no part in public life or the business world, and put the bulk of his energies into the creation and embellishment of Waddesdon and the entertainment of his guests there.

Lord Rothschild is a force to be reckoned with, in finance and in public life. After disagreements in the boardroom he left the family bank in 1980 to set up on his own, and the many ventures in which he is involved range from a part-share in a major conglomerate of French vineyards and ownership of the best plant-centre in London to the purchase of the lease of Spencer House, one of the great eighteenth century houses of London, and its superb restoration between 1985 and 1993. From 1985 to 1991

assistants and experts, presided over an operation almost as complicated, costly and long lasting as the original eight-year creation of Waddesdon under Destailleur, Conder and Sims. And as the dynamo at the centre, instead of Baron Ferdinand, impatient perfectionist, gifted organizer, easily bored, always in a hurry, there is a Rothschild remarkable for his restless energy, his perfectionism, his

Left: The French eighteenth century wall panelling installed in the White Drawing Room was found in storage on the Estate. It was restored by French craftsmen and re-erected in a room designed to match the historic examples of France.

Below: The panelling after restoration.

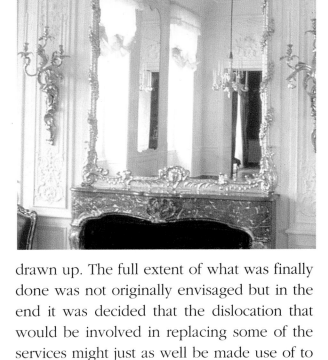

he was a dynamic chairman of the Trustees of the National Gallery and oversaw the addition of the wing given to the Gallery by the Sainsbury brothers in that period. He took over from Mrs. Dorothy de Rothschild as chairman of the Yad Hanadiv Foundation, which has paid for and built the Supreme Court in Jerusalem, among the most impressive of post-war public buildings. From 1992 to 1998 he was chairman of the National Heritage Memorial Fund, one of the five good causes to benefit from the huge success of the new National Lottery. When Mrs. de Rothschild picked him as her heir, it can be surmised that she was consciously selecting the Rothschild who seemed best able to carry Waddesdon into the next century.

The Centenary Restoration

The restoration programme was started in Mrs. de Rothschild's time. In 1984 she suggested in her understated way to Peter Inskip, the architect to Waddesdon, that ...*Perhaps you could do a quick report on the condition of the House...* . This resulted in a five-phase plan for roof repairs. At the time of her death two of these phases had been completed, and plans for the renewal of the services and the fire-precaution system had also been

drawn up. The full extent of what was finally done was not originally envisaged but in the end it was decided that the dislocation that would be involved in replacing some of the services might just as well be made use of to replace all of them, even though the electric wiring, unlike the plumbing and heating, still

A display of over 300 pieces of the Sèvres Starhemberg service installed during the centenary restoration. This service was a gift from Louis XV to Count Starhemberg who had helped to negotiate the wedding of the Dauphin, later Louis XVI, to the Austrian Archduchess Marie-Antoinette.

had some years of useful life to run.

The work that needed to be done was going to take a long time and cost a great deal of money, at the end of which Waddesdon would look very much as it did before work started. This, however useful, was rather depressing as a prospect, and Lord Rothschild and his committee set out to find ways in which they could make a positive mark.

What has emerged, one hundred years after the death of Baron Ferdinand, leaves one in wonder at how little has changed and how much has changed. If the Baron were to resurrect from the Jewish Cemetery at West Ham in London, where he is buried, and to return to Waddesdon, what would he find?

The exterior of the house, fresh from its careful and conservative restoration, looks much

Silk patterns from waistcoats sent from Lyon to Monsieur Judge of Clermont, 3 May, 1778. Drawings and ornamental engravings relating to the decorative arts are part of the extensive collection of pattern books brought together by Baron Ferdinand.

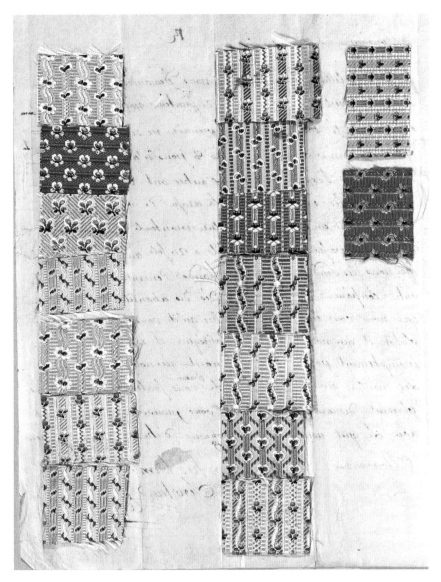

as it did when he died - but now can be illuminated at night. The park is still recognizably the same, allowing for a century of growth, of loss by gale or old age, and of gain by replanting. The gardens are closer than they have been for sixty years to what they were in Baron Ferdinand's time.

Changes inside the House

Inside the house the great rooms on the ground floor would still look recognizably the same to the Baron. All his lovingly col-

lected treasures or, as he liked to call them, 'curiosities' are still there, enriched by the acquisitions of later generations; rooms and contents are still maintained to the impeccable 'Waddesdon standard', but set off now by the latest techniques of lighting, designed for the appropriate illumination of pictures and contents, without glare or damage in terms of conservation. The great table in the Dining Room is still, on special occasions at least, arranged as shown in the photograph in the Baron's Red Book. Gone though, for

many years, are most of the comfortably sha-
peless armchairs and sofas which used to be
interspersed among the treasures for the
convenience of the Baron and his guests
- the inevitable Rothschild difference from
such Victorian furnishings elsewhere being
that they were upholstered with seventeenth

or eighteenth century fabrics of museum
quality, ruthlessly cut to fit.

The biggest changes are on the first floor.
Some of these are conservative. In the Bachelors' Wing the bedrooms have been taken
back to their original nineteenth century mix-

Opposite: The Blue Dining Room with eighteenth century panelling installed during the centenary restoration.

Right: The Wine Cellar is a new addition to the visitors' tour since the centenary restoration. Lord Rothschild's collection of old and rare wines from Château Lafite and Château Mouton-Rothschild is kept in ideal conditions. Wine tastings of Rothschild vintages take place regularly.

ture of treasures, brass bedsteads, and plain wooden bedroom furniture painted white. The Billiard Room has reacquired its original billiard table, and it and the adjacent Smoking Room in the Bachelors' Wing have been restored to the luxurious masculine opulence of the Baron's time.

The rooms on which Lord Rothschild and others have most obviously had an impact are those which used to make up the apartments of Baron Ferdinand himself, and of Miss Alice. These had been much changed in the post-war years. Baron Ferdinand's new apartment above the Morning Room had

been knocked into one big museum room, known as the Long Room; the two rooms of his old apartment had been converted for the display of Sèvres porcelain and musical instruments. Miss Alice's apartment at the other end of the first floor had been redecorated when it was occupied by Mr. and Mrs. James de Rothschild, and then substantially remodelled as living accommodation for National Trust staff.

The two rooms of the Baron's old apartment have now become a room devoted to the history of the Rothschild family and, in the tower, a room in which the Bakst 'Sleeping Beauty' paintings from London are displayed. They bring an unexpected element of the Russian Ballet to Waddesdon - but it is Rothschild not Russian faces which look out from Bakst's exotic decor.

Mrs. Dorothy de Rothschild owned a service of over three hundred pieces of Sèvres porcelain, given by Louis XV to the Austrian Ambassador, Prince Starhemberg, in gratitude for helping to arrange his grandson's marriage to Marie Antoinette; it had passed into Rothschild ownership when it was acquired by Baroness James, wife of one of the original five brothers and grandmother of James de Rothschild. The service was accepted by the Treasury in lieu of death duties, and came on permanent loan to Waddesdon. Its arrival inspired the reconversion of the Long Room to two rooms on the old proportions, one for the display of the Starhemberg service, the other for showing the Razumovsky dessert service, also Sèvres, which was already at Waddesdon.

Above: The rose arbour in the garden at Waddesdon presents a view similar to French gardens such as Bagatelle or La Malmaison on which the rose garden was originally modelled.

Opposite: The Aviary today with its garden and colourful population of many species of rare birds.

At the same time the three rooms of what had been Miss Alice's apartment were remodelled to incorporate French and Flemish boiseries, which had been languishing for years in the stables at Eythrope and elsewhere; some of these had almost certainly been removed from Baron Ferdinand's London house, other panels were left over from the original fitting up of Waddesdon. The panels have been restored, repainted, gilded and (where necessary, to fit their new position) reproduced by the best available contemporary craftsmen in France.

The contrast between these rooms and the other interiors at Waddesdon is a striking one. They are light, sparkling and gay, a twentieth century view of the eighteenth century, carried out on the basis of deeper knowledge of eighteenth century colours and techniques, and quite without the sense of crowded opulence which gives the Baron's interiors their distinctive nineteenth century character, in spite of the eighteenth century elements of which they are mainly composed.

From the new White Drawing Room one can look down on the parterre below, and a dazzling display of colour that would have delighted the Baron and Miss Alice.

The fortunate and rare survival of a set of colour plates showing the gardens at Waddesdon and Eythrope as they were in Miss Alice's time enabled Lord Rothschild's daughter Beth (a member of the Waddesdon Gardens Committee) to make a design for restoring the parterre.

The parterre with spring planting after restoration.

Tradition is respected at Waddesdon and the spirit of the house is maintained when areas are restored. In the 1997 restoration of the Bachelors' Wing, the portrait of Master Braddyll by Reynolds is hung over a Parisian commode of the Transition period.

The Head Gardeners, Christopher Tolley succeeded by Michael Walker, set out with enthusiasm to bring back to life a great Victorian garden with only nineteen gardeners, helped by seasonal volunteers, instead of one hundred and fifty. There is no easy solution, even allowing for the use of modern machinery, slightly simplified design, computer-based records and ingeniously devised methods for mass planting. No modern Lady Warwick is going to wake up to find wind damaged plants magically replaced overnight but, even so, 175,000 plants were bedded out in 1997.

Changes at the Dairy

Important changes have also taken place outside the National Trust boundary, at the Dairy and the Baron's garden next to it. In the Baron's and Miss Alice's time guests conveyed down the hill to the Dairy discovered not just a prettily-tiled room in which cream and butter were made but an entire model dairy farm, combined with rooms for the display of porcelain and other treasures - what, in France at the same period, was called a *'fermette de luxe'*.

On the adjacent site was an elaborately irregular garden laid out with winding ponds and huge rocks (part natural, part artificial) by James Pulham, most celebrated of Victorian creators of rock gardens. The whole complex, Dairy included, had become disused and derelict. Today the Dairy has been resto-

The historical provenance of works of art was of particular importance to Baron Ferdinand. This inventory mark of the French Queen Marie-Antoinette's Office of Works, the 'Garde Meuble de la Reine' is shown on the Queen's table in the Tower Room.

red and added to externally to form a courtyard, and has been partly remodelled internally. The cows have been replaced by secretaries, company directors, bridal couples and guests. New loggias, for dining or drinking, project over the adjacent lake (which is home for more than twenty species of duck) towards the restored rock and water gardens. The complex can be hired, in whole or part, for anything suitable, from a board meeting to a wedding, complete with wedding service.

Continuity within the change

It is all change, but also continuity. The main purpose of the Baron's Waddesdon was for entertaining, and its main purpose is for entertaining still - the instructive entertaining or entertaining instruction of visitors (150,000 to house and gardens in 1997) and the entertaining of the guests who attend events in the Dairy or the Cellars. All in all it is a kind of permanent Baron's Treat, but one which under current conditions has to pay, or help pay, its way.

Waddesdon is still a large and thriving community. In the Baron's time there were about 240 people working in the house, park and gardens, exclusive of farm workers and the staff at Eythrope. Today there are 320, but

Left: This small crystal vase, probably of German origin, was remounted in Paris with very fine mounts at the end of the eighteenth century. It came from the collection of Baron Edmond de Rothschild and is part of the new display in the Bakst Room.

Opposite: Detail of a six-fold Savonnerie screen. The figures of the animals were designed by the French artist Desportes and woven from 1719. At this time screens were popular at the French Court. They were used in the royal dining rooms at Versailles, Marly and Fontainebleau, and given as presents by the King to foreign princes.

the bulk of these are seasonal guides, wardens and garden volunteers; the original 240 were all full time. The difference mainly reflects the change in the numbers of gardeners. The full-time staff in the house itself has not changed all that much, even if employed in different work: thirty-nine under the Baron, forty seven today. There is no longer *...an army coming down the High Street...*, as Mr Hicks describes the workforce returning to the village for their mid-day meal; instead there is a morning and evening irruption of cars from and into the surrounding countryside. Loyalty to, and pride in, Waddesdon remain as strong as ever.

For visitors, coming to Waddesdon remains as memorable an experience as it has ever been, if sometimes an overpowering one; there is a special brand of Waddesdon fatigue, to be observed in those visitors, overcome by the riches which they are trying to absorb, who collapse on the benches thoughtfully provided for them at intervals in the public rooms. Perhaps they feel something of Henry James's distress at *...the gilded bondage of this gorgeous place...* but, like Henry James, they continue to return. There is always something new to discover or talk about in this exotic, unique, baffling, unforgettable and extraordinary place.

It is irresistible to be reminded of Baron Ferdinand's often quoted remarks on the future of his house: *...I fear Waddesdon will share the fate of most properties whose owners have no descendants, and fall into decay. May the day yet be distant when weeds will spread over the garden, the terraces crumble into dust, the pictures and cabinets cross the channel or the Atlantic, and the melancholy cry of the night-jar sound from the deserted towers... .* (17)

Thanks to the high criteria and continuous devotion to Waddesdon of the Rothschilds who have succeeded him, and all who have helped them, the day has not yet arrived; a hundred years after his death it is bedded out

Left: Mask of Apollo, symbol of the sun. A detail of the gilt bronze rail on the roll-top desk made by Riesener for Beaumarchais. The desk is now in the Baron's Room.

Opposite: The coat of arms of the Rothschild family with the Latin motto: *Concordia Integritas Industria*, symbolising the close agreement, moral uprightness and capacity for work of the five Rothschild brothers.

Below: The newly installed floodlight illumination at Waddesdon makes a night visit one of the highlights at the end of every season before the house is 'put to bed' for the winter.

tulips and geraniums, not weeds, which spread over the gardens; the terraces have not crumbled; pictures and cabinets cross the Channel to be restored, not to be sold; and instead of the melancholy cry of the night-jar, mynah-birds in the restored aviary shriek 'Welcome to Waddesdon' to the thousands of visitors who come each year to visit its far-from deserted towers.

NOTES

1. Private Correspondence Baron Ferdinand, The Rothschild Archives, London
2. Private Correspondence Baron Ferdinand, The Rothschild Archives and 'Reminiscences-Ferdinand de Rothschild' unpublished manuscript, Waddesdon Manor Archives
3. Letter dated September 1878, in Letters from Baron Ferdinand de Rothschild to the 5th. Earl of Rosebery. Photocopies in Waddesdon Manor Archives
4. 'Glasgow Evening News' 20.12.1898
5. Private Correspondence Baron Ferdinand, The Rothschild Archives
6. Ferdinand de Rothschild in the introduction to 'The Red Book', p. 3. Waddesdon Manor Archives
7. On Destailleur and his work see: The James A. de Rothschild Bequest at Waddesdon Manor, Architecture and Panelling, Bruno Pons. Philip Wilson 1997
8. Ferdinand de Rothschild in the introduction to 'The Red Book', p.4
9. Ferdinand de Rothschild in the introduction to 'The Red Book', p.9
   The James A. de Rothschild Bequest at Waddesdon Manor, Architecture and Panelling, Bruno Pons. Philip Wilson 1997. See p.74.
10. 'The Bucks Herald', 12th April 1890, Fire at Waddesdon Manor. Gainsborough's picture 'Sisters' depicted Lady Day and the baroness de Noailles, and came from the sale of Mr John Gradam via Agnew into the Collection of Baron Ferdinand.
11. Ferdinand de Rothschild in the introduction to 'The Red Book', p. 3
12. Announcement for Sale by Auction in' The Bucks Herald', 30th May 1874, and Waddesdon Manor Archives (Photocopy)
13. 'The Bucks Herald', 13th July, 1889, The Shah's Visit to Waddesdon
14. 'Baron Ferdinand de Rothschild's Livre d'Or', edited by James Pope-Hennessy, The Roxburghe Club, Cambridge, 1957
15. 'Boyhood Memories, 1902-1911' by Aubrey Cyril Hicks. Photocopy of the manuscript at Waddesdon Manor Archives
16. See note 15
17. Ferdinand de Rothschild in the introduction to 'The Red Book', p.11

BIBLIOGRAPHY

'Waddesdon Manor, Buckingham, The Seat of Baron Ferdinand de Rothschild'. Country Life, August 20, 1898, p. 208-211

'Waddesdon Manor, Buckinghamshire', Charles Latham on English Homes, Country Life, London, 1904, p. 53-58

'Waddesdon Manor, The Rothschild Collection' Apollo, the International Magazine of the Arts, special issue, Vol.CXXXIX, no. 386, April 1994

The Rothschilds at Waddesdon Manor, Mrs. James de Rothschild, Vendôme Press, 1979

Waddesdon's Golden Years 1874-1925, Norman Carr & Ivor Gurney, The Alice Trust, 1996

The Rothschild Gardens, Miriam Rothschild, Kate Garton, Lionel de Rothschild, Gaia Books Ltd., 1996

Les Rothschild Bâtisseurs et Mécènes, Pauline Prevost-Marcilhacy, Flammarion, 1995

PHOTOGRAPHIC CREDITS